W9-AYS-918

DISGUSTING JOBS

BY PATRICK PERISH

EPIC

BELLWETHER MEDIA • MINNEAPOLIS, MN

EPIC BOOKS are no ordinary books. They burst with intense action, high-speed heroics, and shadows of the unknown. Are you ready for an Epic adventure?

This edition first published in 2015 by Bellwether Media, Inc.

No part of this publication may be reproduced in whole or in part without written permission of the publisher. For information regarding permission, write to Bellwether Media, Inc., Attention: Permissions Department, 5357 Penn Avenue South, Minneapolis, MN 55419.

Library of Congress Cataloging-in-Publication Data

Perish, Patrick, author.
  Disgusting Jobs / by Patrick Perish.
    pages cm. – (Epic. Totally Disgusting)
  Summary: "Engaging images accompany information about disgusting jobs. The combination of high-interest subject matter and light text is intended for students in grades 2 through 7"– Provided by publisher.
  Audience: Ages 7-12.
  Audience: Grades 2 to 7.
  Includes bibliographical references and index.
  ISBN 978-1-62617-131-2 (hardcover : alk. paper)
  ISBN 978-0-531-27223-7 (paperback : alk. paper)
  1. Occupations–Miscellanea–Juvenile literature. 2. Job descriptions–Miscellanea–Juvenile literature. I. Title.
  HF5381.2.P427 2014
  331.7'02–dc23
                    2014006604

Printed in the United States of America, North Mankato, MN.

TABLE OF CONTENTS

DISGUSTING BUSINESS!

Cleaning up messes is no party.
But some people have jobs that deal
with spills, smells, and dead animals.
These workers are not afraid
to get dirty.

DEALING WITH WASTE

Sanitation workers collect everyone's gross trash. They take everything from **rotten** eggs to soggy pizza boxes. Their trucks reek from the garbage.

Sort of Disgusting

Totally Disgusting

GROSS-O-METER

Everything that goes down the drain ends up in **sewers**. A horrible stench fills these slimy tunnels. Sewer workers wade through the **wastewater**. They fix cracks and unclog pipes.

HOME SWEET HOME

Sewer workers are not alone in the tunnels. Millions of rats and cockroaches live down there.

GROSS-O-METER

Sort of Disgusting

Totally Disgusting

Hazmat divers swim through **toxic** waters. They clean up **pollution**. They also repair sewer pipes. One tiny hole in their suit would expose them to deadly **diseases**.

GROSS ANIMAL JOBS

Working with animals can be fun. That is, unless they are as flat as pancakes. Roadkill removers scrape animal **carcasses** off the road. Dead critters can get stinky in the summer heat.

GROSS-O-METER

Sort of Disgusting

Totally Disgusting

Sort of
Disgusting

Totally
Disgusting

GROSS-O-METER

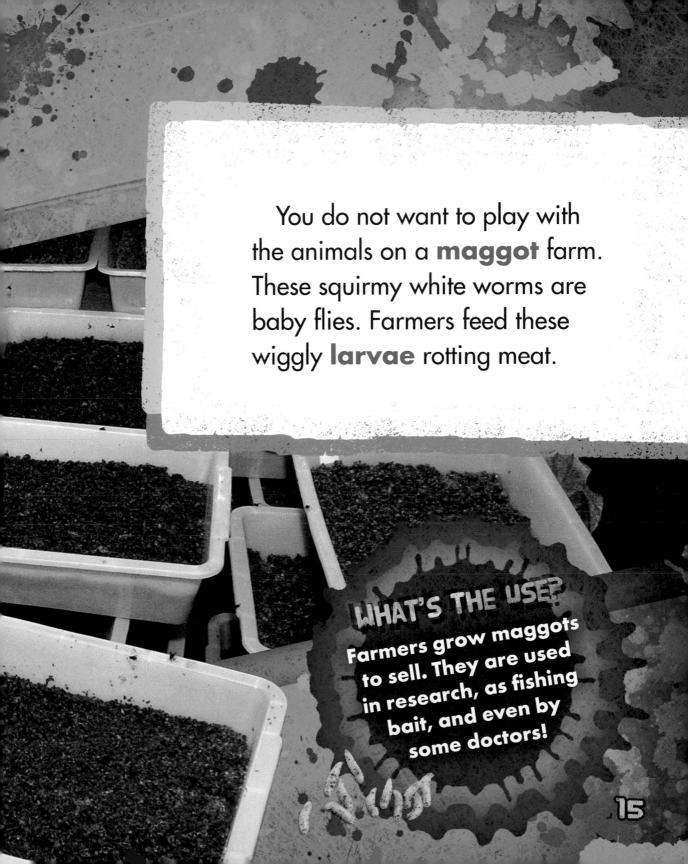

You do not want to play with the animals on a **maggot** farm. These squirmy white worms are baby flies. Farmers feed these wiggly **larvae** rotting meat.

WHAT'S THE USE?
Farmers grow maggots to sell. They are used in research, as fishing bait, and even by some doctors!

HEAVY LOAD

An African elephant can make 300 pounds (136 kilograms) of manure a day!

Caring for giraffes and lions sounds exciting. But every animal poops. Zookeepers shovel mountains of **manure** out of animal cages every day. And you thought taking out the kitty litter was bad?

Sort of Disgusting

Totally Disgusting

GROSS-O-METER

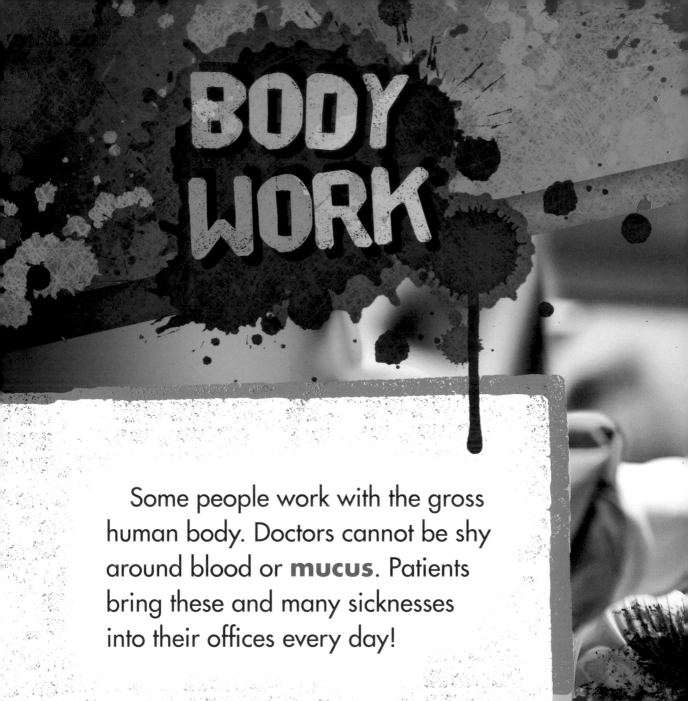

BODY WORK

Some people work with the gross human body. Doctors cannot be shy around blood or **mucus**. Patients bring these and many sicknesses into their offices every day!

Sort of
Disgusting

Totally
Disgusting

GROSS-O-METER

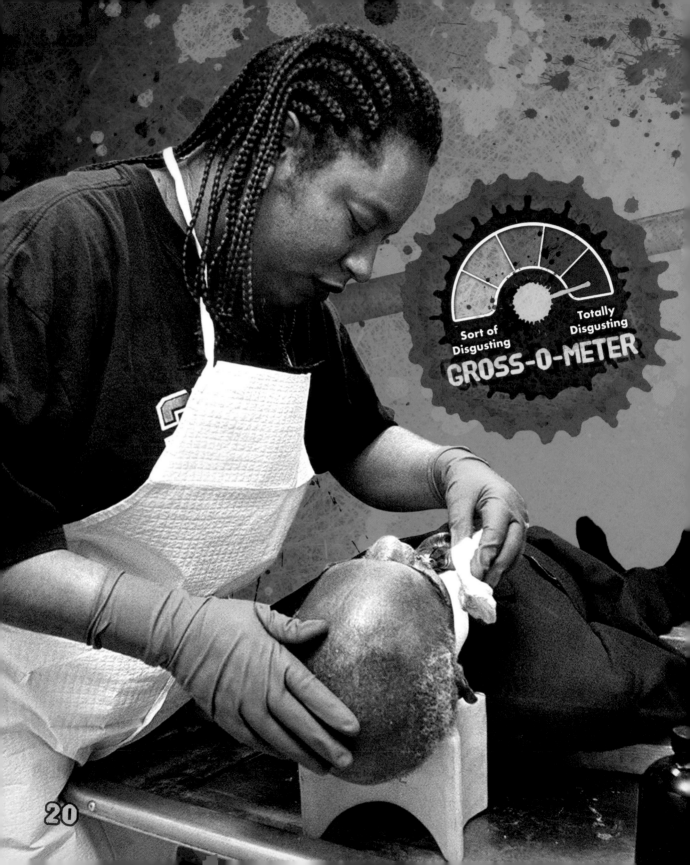

Sort of
Disgusting

Totally
Disgusting

GROSS-O-METER

Morticians cannot be grossed out by dead bodies. They prepare **corpses** for burial. They drain them of blood and gases. That takes a strong stomach!

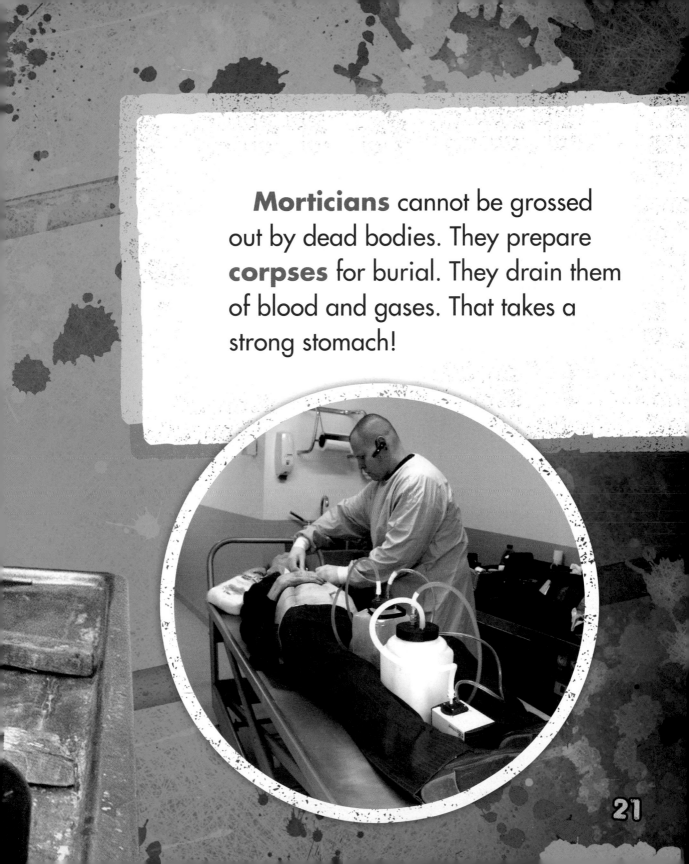

GLOSSARY

carcasses—dead animal bodies

corpses—dead bodies

diseases—sicknesses; diseases can be caused by harmful bacteria.

hazmat—a dangerous substance; hazmat is short for hazardous material.

larvae—insects in the second stage of life; larvae hatch from eggs.

maggot—a baby fly; maggots look like little white worms.

manure—animal dung

morticians—people who prepare dead bodies for burial

mucus—a sticky substance made in the body

pollution—when the environment is dirtied or contaminated; garbage and other harmful substances cause pollution.

rotten—gone bad from decaying

sanitation—cleanliness; good sanitation keeps people healthy.

sewers—tunnels and pipes that hold wastewater

toxic—poisonous; toxic materials are dangerous to people.

wastewater—water that flows into sewers; wastewater contains everything that goes down the drain.

TO LEARN MORE

At the Library

Miller, Connie Colwell. *Disgusting Jobs*. Mankato, Minn.: Capstone Press, 2007.

Perritano, John. *The Most Disgusting Jobs on the Planet*. Mankato, Minn.: Capstone Press, 2012.

Reeves, Diane Lindsey. *Gross Jobs*. New York, N.Y.: Ferguson, 2009.

On the Web

Learning more about disgusting jobs is as easy as 1, 2, 3.

1. Go to www.factsurfer.com.

2. Enter "disgusting jobs" into the search box.

3. Click the "Surf" button and you will see a list of related web sites.

With factsurfer.com, finding more information is just a click away.

INDEX

The images in this book are reproduced through the courtesy of: Tigergallery, front cover (top left); Amber Waterman/ AP Images, front cover (top right); Marcin Balcerzak, front cover (bottom), Scholastic cover; Arun Roisri, pp. 4-5; serato, p. 5 (top right); vadim kozlovsky, p. 5 (middle right); Allison Long/ Newscom, pp. 5 (bottom right), 12-13, 13; Paolo Bona, pp. 6-7; photolinc, p. 8 (small); Boris Horvat/ Getty Images, pp. 8-9; Edward A. Ornelas/ Newscom, pp. 10-11; Herwig Prammer/ Newscom, p. 11; Stringer Shanghai/ Corbis, pp. 14-15; bogdan ionescu, p. 15 (small); NHPA/ SuperStock, pp. 16-17; Portra Images/ Getty Images, pp. 18-19; The Washington Times/ Newscom, pp. 20-21; Platriez/ BSIP/ SuperStock, p. 21.